Journey to Success

Defy the Odds & Realize Your Dreams

Charles Rose Jr.

ISBN – 10: 978-0692773611

ISBN – 13: 0692773614

Intellectual Property of Charles Rose Jr.

Edited by Wayne Purdin, and Crystal Rose Moyer

Cover Design by OctagonLab; Photography by Aaron Cress &
Wade Bruton

Printed in the United States of America

Dedication

This book is dedicated to all those who desire to achieve their dreams.

To my dear parents Charles Rose Sr. and Chassarie Sealy-Bullard. To my stepparents Brian Bullard and Patrice Lundy-Rose. To my siblings Chardonae, Carlos, and Chardre. To my "American Dad," Dr. Byron T. Robinson. To my number one advisor, Rotary President Carol Rolle. To my pastors, Shomari & Jacque White, who have been my spiritual covering.

To the love of my life Katherine Cepeda Vasquez, for encouraging me every day to complete my first "best-selling book." Every day, she told me, **"My love, the world is waiting on this book. Above all, God is waiting. Finish it."**

Acknowledgements

There were so many persons who made the publishing of my first book possible – too many to list all. From the depths of my heart, I am very thankful.

To Curtis Hawn, who helped me get started on my first book take-off back in the summer of 2013. To Chandler Hawn, my college roommate, my engineering study buddy, and my "brother from another mother" for helping me get through college. To my godmother Felena Burrows and her teenage daughter, Serena, for staying up all night to help me edit this book. To Archdeacon Bain, my priest who supported me from the very beginning. To Marian Beane, my "international mother" who always supports my dreams. To the big brother I never had, Travis Greene, for inspiring me to keep pushing even in my hardest times through his music. To the many sponsors and mentors who funded my college education. To all my teachers, from Toddlers Basic Academy, Walter Parker Primary, and Jack Hayward High School. To the UNC Charlotte faculty and staff for helping me achieve my bachelor's degree. To the self-publishing school, for helping me launch my first "best-selling book." To one of the world's most amazing book launch team. To all those who prayed for me.

To my editors, Wayne Purdin & Crystal Moyer, thanks for your time and patience. This book could not have been achieved without you.

I acknowledge everyone who made my first book possible. Thank you.

Table of Contents

Foreword

Life is merely a journey. Once the whistle blows, no one can run the race for you. My dear friend, Charles, reminds us that joy cannot just be reserved for the finish line. **We must embrace every chapter of our life that the Author pens concerning us.**

In this journey, no one lands on the shores of success by accident. Success must be realized before it can ever materialize. To navigate through the terrain of life, it takes persistence, courage, and faith. This book clarifies how success is not merely a place of arrival, but actually a posture for survival. **Prepare to be enlightened, energized, and inspired as you defy all odds and realize your dreams on your journey to success.**

Travis Greene

Introduction

What do you want to be when you grow up?

How many times have you been asked that question? How many times have you asked it of yourself? It's a big question, for sure. As a child growing up, it seems to be the million dollar question, and yet, no one ever tells you how to actually become whatever you aspire to be. Friends, family, and strangers alike, all seem content to respond with a slightly doubting pat on the shoulder and a condescending-yet-polite 'good for you!' As an adult, it often becomes the nagging, sad whisper from your past, reminding you what you wish your future could be.

But what if this question was more than just small talk to fill the empty space in pleasant conversation? What if you could look ahead with a little bit of fear and a lot of determination and know that your dreams truly do still lay ahead of you – real and attainable with a little bit of focused effort?

This book was written to encourage *you* to achieve *your* dreams, no matter what obstacles you may face.

I have been where you are. I have faced the naysayers, the doubters, my own fears, confusion, and of course, financial struggles. But I was blessed to have a mother who pushed me, some mentors who believed in me, and my faith that sustained me despite my meager beginnings and the monstrous obstacles I faced. In this book, I will share the story of my own journey to success. I hope you will be inspired to apply the keys to success I share with you here, so that you, too, can find the courage to embark on your own journey to defy the odds and realize your dreams.

But I am getting ahead of myself. Allow me to tell you a little bit about myself. I began my journey growing up as an underprivileged island boy in Freeport, Grand Bahama, one of 700 islands in the Bahamas.

"But wait. Isn't the Bahamas paradise?" Yes, yes, I know: to the foreigner dreaming of traveling to exotic destinations and the tourist embarking on an international adventure, the Bahamas is considered paradise. But have you ever wondered what life looks like for the average Bahamian local? As is always the case, someone has to work and sacrifice to maintain that "paradise." A lot of high school students, as soon as they graduate, find jobs in the hotel industry, which don't require a college degree. They get jobs in the hospitality and service industry, earning minimum wage. Their work ethic is impressive, but they work long, hard hours for very little pay, and often find themselves stuck in a career with little opportunity for advancement or increase in pay and quality of life. For those locals who have ambitions in the STEM field, medicine, maritime, and the legal profession, a college education is needed.

But many local students only dream of achieving a higher education abroad. Very few take any steps toward this dream, and even fewer actually get there. According to the Migration Policy Institute, only 18.6% of the Caribbean population in the USA have a bachelor's degree or higher, compared to 26.8% of the overall foreign-born population and 28.1% of the native-born population (McCabe, 2011).

There are a number of barriers that hinder the pursuit of higher education for students living in developing countries. The Global Citizen Organization lists 10 major barriers to education on their website. This list offers but a small window of insight into the challenges a child on the island must face and conquer in order to realize his or her dream of a solid education– but it is a start, at least:

1. Lack of funding for education
2. Having no teacher, or an untrained teacher
3. No classroom
4. A lack of learning materials
5. The exclusion of children with disabilities
6. Being the "wrong" gender
7. Living in a country in conflict or at risk of conflict
8. Distance from home to school
9. Hunger and poor nutrition
10. The expense of education (formal or informal fees) (Write to Learn, 2014).

As this list suggests, on the island, life can be very limited. There's only so much you can do. Education is limited. Jobs are limited. Money is limited. Business is limited. Ultimately, growth and development are limited. Even the space and distance are limited. In fact, if you walk too far you'll end up in the water, and you'd better hope you can swim! These limitations, in effect, create a "closed-minded" mentality on the island. As a result, islanders lose hope and stop dreaming. In the same way, many people feel limited in their dreams whether they live on an island or not.

Are you limiting yourself? Have you stopped dreaming because of the limitations around you?

As you'll see in this book, I dreamed of graduating with a Bachelor's of Science degree in Civil Engineering from an accredited university in the USA. But to folks on the island, this was crazy talk. In addition to the limitations I faced to start with, I also had to contend with the limitations others felt I should be putting on myself.

But as you will see, I did embark on my journey to success, defy the odds, and realize my dream of getting my bachelor's in Civil Engineering from an accredited university in the US. And now, I am pursuing my dream to help others to begin their own journey to success to achieve their own dreams. I am sharing my story with you, so that you can write the next story, as so many others already have upon hearing my story. After hearing my story in a UNC Charlotte article (*William States,* 2014), Veronica Dorsett, a Bahamian who studies sculpture in Vancouver, Canada, wrote me the following message:

"Charles, I read a story posted by your school a few months ago and I pretty much carry it with me daily now. I've fought to follow my dreams and now I stand with no money but faith that everything will work out in God's order. I'm heading to Vancouver, Canada to finish my BFA in sculpture. I was granted $10,000 from the Bahamas Ministry of Education last year and then had it taken back because of a mix up. I then had to re-apply and have no clue if they will give it back to me and, like you pointed out in your interview, the Bahamas is always quite last minute. I just thought I'd extend my thanks to you and your story of faith. I think it crosses my mind daily as I wonder if I should give up or get on that plane come August 25th, 2014.

I know it won't be easy and I'm very afraid of the struggle that will ensue but I listened to a talk recently where a psychologist stated that we should go after the things that bring meaning and purpose to our lives.

Just wanted to say thanks. Your story gives me that extra motivation that anything is possible and that all obstacles are a test of faith.

Much blessings to you and your life, Charles. Continue to shine bright and inspire others. I hope and pray that in 2 years, I too will have a story like yours to tell... one of much difficulty but one of deserved success and hard work.

God Bless you and I'm so proud to know you made it! Congratulations!"

Veronica took a step of faith after reading my story and went off to study sculpture in Vancouver Canada. She is still in Vancouver pursuing her bold dreams. Imagine the ridicule she went through growing up in the Bahamas for even having a dream to study "sculpture." Typically, no one on the island does that. They would ask, "How would she make a living?" Not much stock would be placed in someone who studies art or thinks outside the box. Many people consider the study of art - especially sculpture - a waste of time or simply something that only rich people do.

It hurts me deeply when I see a dream lying dormant. When people tell me they wish they had gone to college to be a doctor or lawyer, or that they simply wanted to be a professional athlete or entrepreneur, I ask, *Why didn't you do it?* To so many people, this question is shocking. Dream talks are to be reserved for pleasantries and small talk – no one expects an actual challenge in such an exchange.

What would your answer be? Would you like to move your dreams out of pleasantries and into active, meaningful conversation?

Do you want to talk with someone who takes your dreams as seriously as you do? Who will go beyond a casual 'that would be nice,' and actually help you take steps to achieve your dreams?

Your dreams are important to me. Your dreams are what this book is all about.

Grab a cup of coffee or tea, and let's chat for a few minutes. I'll tell you all about my story – how I went from that poor little island boy to a successful US college graduate with an amazing, international career in the field of my dreams. Be encouraged and inspired by the possibilities you see through my story. Take notes while I share the keys I used on my journey to success. And then, let's work together to get you started on your own next steps toward defying the odds and realizing your dreams - whatever they may be.

My story is just the starting point. Together, we will make your story the next story.

I can't wait to hear it.

The world is waiting on your story. Don't delay. Read on. Be encouraged. You have a story that the world needs to hear. Your story is the next story.

Part 1: The Journey

Prologue: Dinner in Monaco

Sitting down at the table at a restaurant in the City-State of Monaco, I felt like the happiest college graduate in the world. I had just graduated with honors at UNC Charlotte, where I was fortunate enough to have the honor of delivering the student graduation speech. Now I was on an all-expense-paid trip on a Mediterranean Highlights Contiki Tour in Europe. My family and friends knew that it was my dream to travel the world someday, so they went in together to send me on this trip as a graduation gift. It was perfect!

Before this trip, I had only seen these places on TV and read about them in books. Now I was finally experiencing them in person. The tour started in Madrid, Spain where a group of us gathered for the many adventures ahead. We were from different countries such as the USA, Canada, Guyana, South Africa, Sri Lanka, Japan, and of course The Bahamas! In Spain, we visited Madrid, Zaragoza, and Barcelona! Every day, we went sightseeing and visited many famous places, like the *Palacio Real* (the royal palace) in Madrid, straight to the *Basilica of the Sagrada Familia* in Barcelona. At night, we experienced the Spanish dance clubs, where I was introduced to the world of salsa dancing. It was a memorable experience! The closest I came to visiting these places before was in my dreams! I kept pinching myself as a reminder that I wasn't dreaming, especially when tasting the *muy delicioso* (very delicious) food!

At this point, we had already seen Spain and France. Now we were visiting Monaco, one of the wealthiest cities in the world, known for the prestigious Grand Prix motor race, and the famous Monte Carlo Casino, a place most people only see on TV - like in James Bond movies. In order to live in Monaco, you need to be REALLY wealthy and have at least 500,000 euros sitting in a Monaco bank account at all times.

The entire tour group was at the dinner table at a restaurant called "U Cavagnetu," when one of my new friends from Canada, Jia, put me in the spotlight. She got everyone quiet and said to me, "Share your story, Charles! We want to hear it!" I thought to myself, *Why did I drink that French wine the night before? Crap, I must have told her my story. The plan was to just have fun in Europe and keep it low key.* Everyone stared at me waiting for me to speak. …Hesitantly, I began.

Chapter 1 – In the Beginning

My story began at a very different table in a different country in a quite different environment. At a very young age, my mother and older sister, Chardonae, lived with my grandmother in Freeport, Bahamas, because we could not afford to live on our own. When I was around 7 years old, my mother sat Chardonae and me down at the table in a local Pizza Hut Restaurant, and showed us a map of the world. My mom told us, "Find the Bahamas on this map." We were very excited to show off our geography knowledge and quickly pointed out the Bahamas situated in the Atlantic Ocean, right next to the east coast of Florida and right above the Caribbean Sea. She then asked, "My children, did you see that?"

We were clueless. The answer to her question seemed obvious but vague at the same time.

Finally, she replied, "The Bahamas is only a dot on the map. Some maps these days do not even show the Bahamas. My children, there is a whole world out there for you to explore. Never limit yourself to the Bahamas. Get your college degree. Travel the world and make your name great."

"WOW Charles, your mom was right! Look where you are now, from the Bahamas to Monaco," said Lauren from Australia.

Mom continued, "How do you want others to remember you when you die? Don't get stuck at home, in the closed-minded 'island' mentality that limits how successful you become. Home will always be home, you can always come back if you need to." My mother wanted us to achieve what she never had a chance to do. Right after high school, she started working and then my sister was born, so she never got to pursue her dreams. She didn't want the same thing happen to us.

At a very young age, we didn't expect that answer, and were wondering, *Why is mommy trying to get rid of us already?*

However, we never forgot that powerful moment with Mom at the table, when she showed us the map of the world. My sister and I thought about it constantly and dreamt of all the cool places to visit around the world. Maybe one day we would travel to London, USA, or Ecuador. Or maybe China, since "everything" was made in China.

Chapter 2 – Growing Up

At the dinner table in Monaco, I paused so we could enjoy our food, but my friends were so captivated by my story that I had to continue, even though my food was getting cold.

Mom always reminded us, while growing up, to be open-minded and get ready to "go off," or leave the nest. To ensure our detachment from our comfort zone, she even threatened us that she would get a small one-bedroom home with tiles on the floor. "So don't get too comfortable," she would often remind us. "Cold tiles are not comfortable to sleep on." People thought she was cold and harsh, but she knew what she was doing. She knew we had an assignment to fulfill, and in order to achieve it, we had to experience a level of discomfort. We had to get out of the closed-minded island mentality.

It didn't take us too long to become sold out on our mother's ideas. We were convinced that we were going to college, whatever that was. We were convinced that we were going to travel the world, which seemed impossible to everyone. We were convinced that we were going to be great. This motivated us to go above and beyond in our academics and extra-curricular activities. By the time we entered junior high, Chardonae and I had afterschool and summer jobs and were saving for our future. We had an entrepreneurial spirit from an early age. We started our own business selling overpriced snacks from our lunch bags. We had extra special snacks, or, at least, this is what we convinced others they were. However, this didn't last too long; we were caught by a school administrator and had to stop our sales because we were not "authorized vendors."

Hearing this part of the story, everyone laughed at the dinner table in Monaco. Warren, from South Africa, asked, "Did you get in trouble?"

Rocco from Australia, said, "Shhh, don't ruin the story; let Charles finish telling us his story."

I laughed and told my friends, "We didn't get in trouble, since we shut down the business; but we did find other legal ways to generate money, which I will share with you soon."

While many of our friends used all of their money to buy toys, video games, clothes, and other stuff, we saved up for this thing called, "College." Our friends on the island could not understand why; in all honesty, neither did we fully understand what we were doing. We just knew that we were "going off" to college someday, or at least that's what Momma said, and it sure sounded good! Many people considered us different since we preferred to save our money for college rather than buying toys.

Come to think about it, we actually enjoyed being different. We spent many hours imagining our future. We would create the future we imagined through our toys and later virtual worlds on the computer through games like the Sims and Habbo Hotel. Whatever we didn't have, we created it. In fact, I spent most of my time designing and building mini structures out of cardboard, plastic, and scrap paper, such as houses and malls for Chardonae's dolls.

I remember designing and building a model Burger King and Kentucky Fried Chicken. It was so complex and well-designed for my age that one of the owners of the local franchises in the Bahamas, Mrs. Patrice Cooper, rewarded me with cash and free meals at Burger King. I will never forget that moment! I suddenly thought to myself, "Hmm... If I can make money and get free food creating fake developments and fake buildings, imagine how much money I can make creating real developments and real buildings." These early experiences were the beginnings of my passion for design and construction, which would ultimately lead me into a Civil Engineering & Construction career.

In the summer of 2005, after 7th grade, I had my first full-time job working in landscaping and condominium renovations with my uncle Henry aka *Pancake*, the husband of my mother's sister, Mary, making $65 a week. That summer was a turning point for me. It opened my eyes to the importance of working to make money. I would look for any small and odd jobs I could do. I worked part-time after school sweeping floors, taking out trash, and cleaning windows, in a local barbershop a few blocks away from my home, making around $5 per hour. You may think $5 per hour isn't a lot, but for me, that was gold. I treasured that money like nobody's business, as we would say back home. The following two summers, I worked at Burger King, flipping burgers, pumping drinks, and cleaning, where I made $110 per week. To me, I hit the jackpot!

"WOW, Charles, you were ambitious from a young age," said Shannon, my new American travel buddy.

But I also realized I could not spend the rest of my life doing that job. In the summer of 2008, I worked at Bahamas Telecommunications - a phone company - filing papers as a summer intern making $90 per week. To me that was a drop in pay, but it taught me a lot about running a business, which was invaluable. While in high school, I gained work experience shadowing engineers in the engineering inspections department of the Grand Bahama Port Authority, a private development company in Freeport. My last job before my senior year in high school was working as a summer intern at Riviere Associates, a land surveying and site design company in the Bahamas making $200 per week! This was a huge deal for me, because it was the most I had ever made in my life! I felt rich because I did not have any bills at the time! Minimum wage on Grand Bahama at that time was approximately $175 per week. Imagine having to take care a family of 3-5 persons with so little! Little did I know of the huge college costs that lay ahead. From age 11 up until I graduated from high school, I was able to save a total of approximately $1,550.73. Thankfully, I was able to save just about every penny because of a deal my father and I made. My father agreed to cover all of my expenses, as long as I saved all of my income for college. Of course, most of you know that $1550.73 is not enough to pay for a college education in the USA. I, however, did not. Not yet, at least. I worked hard and saved for all those years to go to college, having faith that it would pay off.

Meanwhile, I always maintained stellar academic performance in my schoolwork, and received many academic awards. My life at school was a job in itself. I got involved with many extracurricular activities such as the Interact Club, in which we did lots of community service; the book club; the school band, playing the clarinet and tenor saxophone for Junkanoo (a native Bahamian music and dance festival); engineering bridge competitions; the school council; and many more. Somehow, I always found myself being promoted to leadership roles, though I didn't really ask for them. I just wanted to learn and make a positive difference wherever I went. While in high school, my three largest roles were Headboy (equivalent to student body president), Interact President, and Interact District Governor of Rotary District 6990, which includes Florida and Grand Bahama Island. Mrs. Shantell Thompson (Shantell Rolle, at that time), one of my teachers and the Interact Club Advisor, was very instrumental in pushing me into these leadership roles. She helped to break me out of my comfort zone.

Believe it or not, before high school, I was a very shy guy. You couldn't get me to speak in front of an audience at one point of time.

One of my Contiki friends, Tharsha, from Sri Lanka said, "NO WAY, Charlie, you were not shy." I told her believe it or not, I was. I continued my story in the midst of amazed faces.

My parents broke me out of this shyness. My mother would sign me up for many different programs in the community whether I wanted to be a part of it or not. She pushed me outside into the neighborhood to make friends and would encourage me to invite friends over. She would always stress the point, "You can't make it being book smart only. You need to be street smart. My son, in order to excel in this world, you need to be well-rounded." One time I decided to stay in my room to hide myself from the world, and my mom got her screwdriver and removed my door off the hinges. I had no bedroom door for almost two years. I was forced to interact with people. My dad was a bit calmer than Mom about me being shy, but he would always remind me, "Son, remember, shy guys always get the last say or NO say at all."

Everything changed when I became a part of the Interact Club at Jack Hayward High School. Mrs. Thompson encouraged me to speak up and share what was on my mind. While I was in the 10th grade, the current Interact Club President at the time, in her own words, "cracked under pressure." She simply stopped showing up to meetings, leaving the club without leadership, like a ship without a captain. The vice president was already out of the picture, because he too had other things going on in his life. I found that it hurt me to see the club without leadership, and that I was willing to do just about anything to keep the club running. For this, for the first time in my life, I was willing to step out of my comfort zone, even though I was scared and didn't have a clue what to do. I had to do something! Since the president was absent, I offered to moderate the next meeting. To add to my anxiety, we were scheduled to have as guest speaker, Past President Billy Jane, from the Rotary Club of Lucaya.

When I realized what I offered to do, I was like *Oh my God what did I get myself into!* I was so nervous; I couldn't sleep that night. Suddenly I had an idea to ask one of my closest friends, Cynthia, to co-host the meeting with me. Thank goodness, she agreed because I didn't know what I was going to do by myself! Cynthia and I were great moderators and the session was a success! We kept the audience interested by telling jokes, short stories, and asking trivia questions. It showed us who was paying attention and who wasn't! We had a very successful meeting with a good showing – the room was packed! Mrs. Thompson was very pleased with the meeting and commended Cynthia and me for a job well done. From that point forward, people called me "Mr. Interact" because of my newly formed passion to serve my community. That semester, I ended up moderating every meeting thereafter, and speaking at the annual island-wide Interact Club Awards on behalf of my school's club as "Acting President." At this event, I began networking with many other young leaders from the Interact Clubs at other schools and with many prominent Rotary Club members in our community. These successes inspired a newfound self-confidence, and were the catalysts that further sparked my desire to achieve greatness. I was no longer the shy boy who didn't want to be involved in any activities. Instead of focusing on myself and what others thought about me, I adapted the famous Rotary International motto, "Service Above Self." I loved what I did and worked with my team to get hundreds of students involved in community service projects through Rotary and Interact both in Florida and the Bahamas. There was no more "Mr. Shy Guy" for me.

Throughout all of this, Mom continued reminding us to always keep an open-mind and to get ready to go off to college. At this point, we understood that she only wanted us to live a better life than her and Dad. She would say, "I'm working three jobs at the printing office, waitressing at the restaurant, and braiding hair on the side to make ends meet. Your daddy is a bus driver. I don't want you to fall into the same trap as we did. Don't work hard, work smart. You don't have to make the same mistakes as your daddy and me in order to learn. You can learn from our mistakes." These words resonated with Chardonae, and with me. We faced our futures with confidence – thanks to Mom, we knew exactly what *not to do* in order to avoid getting stuck in a rut. What we didn't realize, however, was that we still didn't know what exactly *to* do in order to pursue the success we sought.

Chapter 3 – Struck by a Coconut

The years were passing by very quickly, and soon I found myself in the summer before 12th grade. Suddenly, reality hit me hard in the head. It was as though I had been relaxing in a hammock between two coconut trees and, suddenly, a coconut fell from the tree and struck me. But instead of a coconut, I was struck with a stark realization - if I was going to go off to college after high school, somehow, I needed to figure out how to get in. I was completely clueless! Naturally, I went to my mom and asked her.

She replied, "I don't know son, google it; I didn't buy a computer and give you access to the Internet for you to play. You better get on that computer and google it!"

So I got on the computer and googled myself to the next level.

This is when the application process started; this is when the "rubber met the road." By this time, my passion from my youth for designing and building stuff for my sister's dolls had matured through several opportunities I had of shadowing a few engineers with the Grand Bahama Port Authority Engineering Department. I knew that I wanted to study Civil Engineering. So, that summer, I googled many civil engineering colleges on the Internet to find out how to apply. From my research, I discovered that I wanted to study at an accredited American university for four years. Therefore, I had to take the SAT (Standard Aptitude Test).

Everything was new to me at that point. Many questions flooded my mind. How do I choose a college? How do I apply? Where do I take the SAT? I was fortunate to be introduced to a friend of Mr. Derreck Farquharson (one of my first mentors), who was a chemical engineer, and his daughter who was studying engineering at MIT. He was a very wise man. I learned from him in 3 minutes three questions that got me to college, through college, and through life up to now and beyond. He taught me to always remember three questions (in order) when solving a problem. I call them the 3 W's:

1. What do I know?
2. What can I find out?
3. Who can I ask?

My problem was, "How can I go off to college in the USA?" So Mr. Farquharson's friend process went like this:

1. **What do I know?**
   I knew I was going to college to study Civil Engineering at an accredited institution in the USA.

2. **What can I find out?**
   Through my research, I found out many of the crucial requirements such as needing passing scores on the SAT, application deadlines, preparation tips, and all the costs associated with it - Ouch!

3. **"Who can I ask?"**
   Over the next couple of months, I spent most of my time asking college graduates like my teachers, engineers, and anyone who I came in contact with all about their college experience. I would ask them questions such as, "How did you choose your college? Are there any scholarships available? What advice would you give to me for college?" Meanwhile, I was preparing for college by taking the SAT, and applying to about five universities.

"She knew she had to let us go in order to let us grow."

Thankfully, my mother had been adamant about teaching my sister and me the importance of being self-reliant. It wasn't that she didn't want us to seek help when we needed it. She just wanted us to control our own future, not depend on anyone - including her and Dad - to accomplish our goals. As soon as I was tall enough to look over the countertop and washing machine, I was washing my own dishes, preparing my own food, and doing my own laundry. These duties began in my elementary school years. Whenever my sister and I needed an application form filled out for an activity, Mom allowed us to fill it out ourselves, and then she checked it before signing to make sure it was done right. We began filling out all our application forms from elementary school; by the time we were in high school, we didn't need any help filling out our application forms; all we needed was a parent's signature, since we were underage. We couldn't believe how many of our friends didn't know how to fill out an application form. Again, many of Mom's colleagues and family criticized her about being "too harsh"; however, she knew that she had to let us go in order to let us grow. I filled out applications to the American colleges I dreamed of attending with confidence and great skill.

My research and preparation process went very well, except for one thing – my finances.

Chapter 4 – The Biggest Coconut

As I confidently went about the business of applying to the schools I dreamed of attending, the coconut tree struck once again. But this time, an even larger coconut dropped, hitting me in the head and giving me an even larger reality check. If I was going to college, how was I going to pay for it? Being a big dreamer, the annual expenses for my top university picks were anywhere from $30,000 to $50,000. My parents' salary was nowhere even close to my annual college expenses. The application process alone depleted nearly all of my life savings.

Working as hard as I did to earn and save money for college for years growing up, you would think I had a lot of money, right? Well, as an island boy, no matter how hard you work, your dollars will never go far, especially in the American world. As I mentioned, I had only saved $1550.73 in all of that time. SAT prep materials and classes cost me $300. The test itself cost about $140. I applied to five schools, the application fee for each ranging between $50 and $75. What was even more expensive was paying $200 to have my Bahamas high school transcript converted to U.S.-equivalent grades, and then paying about $100 to have it sent to each school. Before I knew it...I was broke. Yes, that's right. Nearly my entire life savings was gone, before I even chose which school I would attend.

Then my first letter from the universities I applied to came in from the University of North Carolina at Charlotte, which appeared in my email around my birthday in March 2010. When I first saw that email, my heart was beating so fast, I felt like it would jump out of my chest! I opened the email nervously, but then jumped for joy. I was accepted at University of North Carolina at Charlotte! I was very ecstatic. Since I received my first acceptance letter from UNC Charlotte, I decided to attend this university. I didn't even bother spending any more time and money into the other universities that I had applied to. My sole purpose now became to just get into UNC Charlotte.

At the time, the annual estimated cost for out-of-state international students to study at UNC Charlotte was $30,000 per year! Many of my family and friends thought it was absurd and inconsiderate for me to choose a school that expensive. They told me it would be far better to begin by taking classes at the local College of the Bahamas at night, while working a job in the daytime to pay my way through college. "It would be far easier and better to do it this way. If you are to go off to school, choose something less expensive; don't choose a top expensive school, unless they are giving you a full scholarship beforehand." These were the words I heard from many of my family and friends. Two of my college-educated family members with master's degrees even told me I was not making a wise decision by choosing an expensive, reputable school. They told me they started out at the College of the Bahamas, and that's what I should do in order to be successful. I respectfully and firmly told them, "Just because you did it that way, does not mean that it's the best way for me. I've got to follow my dreams." Well, they got offended, and accused me of being rude.

"You told them, Charles!" exclaimed one of my Contiki friends, Roma from Guyana. I told them I honestly had no intentions of being rude to my family, I believe they had good intentions as they felt they knew best. They all laughed and wanted to hear the rest of the story.

I applied for just about every scholarship available to help with the astronomical costs. I naively believed that I would be able to pick, choose, and refuse scholarships because of my good grades and community service record - I had no idea how highly competitive scholarships can be, and how difficult it can be to get one. No matter what it took, I so desperately wanted to study at UNC Charlotte. I couldn't see myself studying at the College of the Bahamas (COB). COB offers mostly 2-year associate programs in Grand Bahama. It had no Civil Engineering program. UNC Charlotte, on the other hand, had a 4-year accredited Civil Engineering program that was competitive with many other top engineering universities. Students who receive a UNCC Civil Engineering degree immediately find jobs upon graduation in the USA and all around the world. My current employer, Blythe Construction Inc., actually gave me a job offer about three months before graduating from UNCC. COB may have been the perfect fit for others' dreams, but it was not the right path for me to achieve mine. Though it was different, and some didn't understand, I knew I wanted to pursue the 4-year Civil Engineering program at UNCC.

I remember emailing the engineering scholarship department at UNC Charlotte after getting my acceptance letter. I received a warm email reply from LeeAnn Parker. She sent me a very sweet email informing me that the department unfortunately would not be able to assist me at the time. The department only gave scholarships after completing at least one year at UNC Charlotte. I thanked her for her time and told her I looked forward to meeting her soon. LeeAnn became a key figure in my life. I'm so glad I kept a good relationship with her. She and her husband got me my first full-time engineering job, since her husband, Sampson, was a Site Superintendent at Blythe Construction.

Though it may have been a bit painful and shocking at first, getting struck by the coconut was a good thing. I needed that reality check to get going. It prompted me to begin googling my way through things online, and asking others for advice. It led me to me learning to always ask myself the 3 W's (What do I know? What can I find out? Who can I ask?). As a result, I managed to take my SATs, get accepted at UNC Charlotte, and get the scholarship application process started. But, there were still lots of questions to be answered. What would happen after high school? Would all of my plans work out? How *was* I going to get all that money?

Chapter 5 – I Need Mo' Money!

It seemed like time was moving very fast. Jack Hayward High School graduation day came rolling in on June 10, 2010. For having the highest grade point average of my graduating class, I was awarded the honor of being Valedictorian. In my graduation speech, I compared our journey of high school to that of a rocket ship launching into space. I still have a copy of this speech. Here is an excerpt from the beginning of my speech. I opened with an analogy for my fellow graduates:

> *"Les Brown once said, 'Shoot for the moon. Even if you miss, you'll land among the stars.'*
>
> *Class of 2010, we have certainly shot for the moon! And I say this because there are 200 of us who made it here today! Our graduating class had one of the lowest dropout rates. Fellow graduates you should be proud of this great accomplishment.*
>
> *I consider our journey of high school years similar to the journey of a rocket launching into space.*
>
> *In order for rockets to launch, there must be an action, which results in an equal and opposite reaction – We took action in our studies; now we are launching from graduation to the next phase of our lives. Meanwhile, there is a force called gravity; it's trying to pull the rocket back to earth - This force represents all of our haters trying to pull us down. When rockets are launching, many people are watching, which goes to show that people are always watching our actions."*

I was literally shooting for the moon with all of my big plans! Let's face it, I needed mo' money! The Notorious B.I.G. has a song called "Mo Money Mo Problems." For me, it was more like *Mo Money NO Problems.*

For achieving the highest cumulative grade point average, I received a $2,000 scholarship from the Grand Bahama Port Authority. This was awesome and certainly a help toward my goal of $30,000. I was confident that this $2,000 would be the first of many scholarships that summer.

However, the month of June went by and I still only had $2,000 toward my balance. I found out that I was denied one of the largest scholarships I had applied for. Instead of being discouraged, I still kept my faith in God and believed that, somehow, I would be awarded the other scholarships I applied for. I was able to secure a job at Riviere Associates (Land & Engineering Surveyors). I was fortunate to secure this job two summers in a row, through one of my best high school teachers, Mrs. Beverley Hinds. The team at Riviere was very supportive of my dreams, unlike many of the naysayers on the island. They allowed me to prepare for university during work hours, of course in moderation. I was able to take extra time during my lunch breaks to check on scholarship applications, and to take time off to travel to Nassau, Bahamas, to get my U.S. student visa. Through this job, I was able to save enough money to buy a plane ticket and earn money to use on books or living expenses my first semester at UNC Charlotte. I am still thankful for the opportunities and support I received through the awesome team at Riviere during my time there.

But still - despite all my planning and efforts - the end of July came and went, and I was still $28,000 away from being able to pay my $30,000 balance at UNCC. A few more of the scholarships I applied for denied my applications. In addition, the Bahamas Government stopped the student loan program that year due to many students failing to repay the Government. Also, banks in the Bahamas changed their student loan eligibility policy that same year; only 3rd or 4th year students were eligible to receive a student loan. Things had changed in the Bahamas with getting money for higher education. It did not bode well for me.

July 2010 had been a very challenging month for me, but my faith in God increased, and my relationship with Him grew closer. He was the only one I could trust, the only One who understood me, and the only One who believed in me. I was at a point where I could not understand why nothing seemed to be working for my good. Scholarships were turning me down; family and friends thought I was crazy for even considering such a dream. There were many deserving students for scholarships, but I thought that certainly I should be one of them. I had worked so hard all my life for this moment, yet I couldn't see a clear path ahead to go off to university.

Through all of the struggles I faced that summer, I believe God spoke to me through three songs to encourage me to keep fighting for my crazy dream:
1. "Empty Me" by William Murphy
2. "I Give Myself Away" by William McDowell
3. "Breakaway" by Kelly Clarkson

"Empty Me" reminded me to empty all the things out of me that were not of God, such as doubt, lack, failure, and discouragement. "I Give Myself Away" encouraged me to dedicate my life to God for Him to use me as He pleased. "Breakaway" helped me to realize that I had to break away from everything I was accustomed to, and take the risk of following my dreams. Few things in life can speak to the heart like music can - I am so thankful I had access to each of these songs to help me through that difficult time.

"You won't be the first, and you won't be the last to make it through financial challenges. You will survive."

Rotarian President, Carol Rolle, my Interact Club advisor at the time, encouraged me and taught me about faith. To this day, Mrs. Rolle is truly a blessing in my life. She encouraged me to ignore the naysayers, and follow my dreams. She shared with me the struggles her daughter Shasheena experienced while she was in college in the USA. Every semester, Shasheena had a financial struggle, but God would always come through right on time. Carol reminded me what my mother always said, "You won't be the first, and you won't be the last to make it through financial challenges. You will survive."

To be completely honest, I had no idea what I was getting myself into. I had no idea how my story would play out. Somehow, I just believed that everything would work out. Carol Rolle and my stepmother Patrice Rose recommended writing letters requesting financial assistance for university, and delivering them to businesses in the community. I felt it was a great idea, but nearly every business I sent the letter to either said no or never responded.

Patrice Cooper, however, was one of the few who said "yes." Mrs. Cooper was the same lady who had rewarded me with cash and free meals when I designed and built a model of her Burger King & Kentucky Fried Chicken store in my younger days (Chapter 2). She told me she had already exceeded her planned giving funds, and that two of her children were abroad in college; however, she also said that she wanted to help me, even if it was a small amount. She and her husband, Paxton Cooper, blessed me with a $500 check, and told me to use the money for whatever I needed. I was also fortunate to have the assistance of my stepfather, Brian Bullard, who assisted me with obtaining my U.S. student visa. He had obtained his bachelor's degree in the USA, and was a bit more familiar with the process than my other friends and family were. Gifts like these from my stepfather and the Coopers were rays of sunshine in that bleak summer full of so much rejection. Even though I was still left facing a hefty balance to pay, God was able to use these gifts to encourage me, and to remind me that He would make a way, even where I saw none.

After completing high school, I certainly learned that being the top student does not always get you the top scholarship awards. As I mentioned previously, I had always envisioned myself picking, choosing, and refusing scholarships immediately after I graduated high school. But for some reason, my story was not playing out that way. My only hope left was my faith in God. In God is where I found peace in the midst of it all.

There was still one thing I needed two weeks before the start of my enrollment at UNC Charlotte. I still needed money, and I needed a lot more of it to accomplish my dreams. This led me to doing something very crazy on the island.

Chapter 6 - Crazy Island Boy

About two weeks before the start of my enrollment, I did the craziest thing I had ever done! With the nearly depleted life savings I had left, I purchased a ONE-WAY airline ticket to Charlotte, North Carolina in hopes of pursuing my dreams of attaining a Bachelor of Science degree in Civil Engineering. Nearly everyone who knew my story thought I was crazy! I was an island boy going to an unknown city I had never visited with only a small fraction of the funds I needed to cover my university fees. One of my dear high school teachers panicked. "Oh Lord! What crazy thing is Charles getting himself into now?" she worried. Many people thought I was a foolish boy. For those of you who are accustomed to taking risks and going on adventures, jumping on a boat, train, or plane, please understand where I'm coming from. This is a big deal for an island boy living in a country where some people have never left the island in their entire lives. Some islanders have never even visited the other end of the island. I'm sure many of you from developing countries can somewhat relate to what I am talking about.

One of my Contiki friends from Australia, Ryan, exclaimed, "You *are* kind of crazy, Charles!" We all laughed and I told him I certainly might be.

A day before my flight was scheduled to go to Charlotte, North Carolina, I remember going to my home church, Christ the King, in Freeport, Bahamas on August 15th 2010. Father Bain, my priest, invited all of the students who were going to college in the Fall of 2010 to the altar for prayer.

At this point, I was almost running to the altar because I needed every prayer possible with my situation. Let's face it; I needed a miracle to raise $30,000 in a very short amount of time. My international student orientation at UNC Charlotte was on August 17th, 2010. Father Bain prayed for us and asked us to face the congregation. He then asked us to share our name and what college or university we would be attending. Man oh man, at this point, my heart was jumping out of my chest! It was pretty much on the floor.

I didn't sign up for this. I thought we were only coming to the altar for prayer, not to also introduce ourselves and what school we were attending. I can still hear those thoughts going through my mind. *O-M-G! Boy, are you going to lie in the front of the church congregation saying you are going off to UNC Charlotte when you don't even have the $30,000 for your school fees? It would be better off to play it safe and smart by telling them you're going to the College of the Bahamas where it would be easier to afford.* We all faced the congregation, about seven students total. Thankfully, I was on the opposite end of where the microphone started, and I had some time to get my thoughts together before it got to me. What would I say?

Finally, it was my turn. I held the microphone tight in my hands and intensely stared at the audience. What should I say? UNC Charlotte or College of the Bahamas? I opened my mouth and spoke into the microphone declaring...

> *"My name is Charles Rose Jr. I will attend the University of North Carolina at Charlotte."*

At this point, my story also caught the attention of the waiter in the restaurant in Monaco. He stood by the table listening intently to our conversation.

The church congregation proudly applauded when they heard my answer; but I'm sure there were persons in the audience who were mostly shocked because they knew I had no money for college. I could hear the negative voice in my head saying, *What are you gonna do now? They are really going to know that you're a liar if you fail at your attempts to study at UNC Charlotte.* I chose to tell this voice *SHUT UP*; but in reality, I didn't know what I was going to do and what was going to happen. Little did I know how powerful this public announcement was. By actually publicly declaring my intent, I was cementing my determination. It no longer was a secret wish I hoped and prayed for. It was now more real because I said it.

The day of my departure finally arrived. On August 16th 2010, at the Grand Bahama International Airport, as I was preparing to check in to my flight to Charlotte, I had a big choice to make, one that would change my life forever. Should I play it safe by staying on the island and going to the College of the Bahamas? OR should I take a risk by going to Charlotte hoping everything would work out? I remember this day clearly. Many of my family and friends were at the airport seeing me off, not knowing what would happen. I know many of them weren't sure if I would actually go through with it and get on that plane.

Before I went through the departure gate terminal, Mrs. Rolle told me she had something for me. I honestly thought she was about to surprise me with a $30,000 scholarship check. To my surprise, she ran to her car and brought back a book. It was called, *Those Who Trust in the Lord Shall Not Be Disappointed* by Peggy Joyce-Ruth. Little did I know at the time how important this gift was.

As I walked through the first departure gate at the airport, I looked back again at my family and friends. Some were in tears - a mixture of joy and sorrow. My mother and Mrs. Carol Rolle just smiled. Somehow, they were at peace with my choice of leaving the island on crazy faith. I felt like I was walking on water. I had stepped out of the boat for the first time in my life. Many of my family and friends could not believe what I was doing and saw no way it could work. Some even warned me again that I would fail if I went off to school uncertain of how my school fees would be paid.

After being cleared through U.S. immigration, I sat in the airport terminal waiting on my flight to Charlotte. While staring at the roof dreaming about my unknown future, I remembered my new book and decided to pull it out.

Shortly after opening the book, I heard my name being called over the PA system. "Charles Rose Jr., please report to the gate agent counter." *Why were they calling me?* I quickly moved along to the departure gate agent. She said, "Mr. Rose, you received an envelope from the front."

Immediately, I tore open the envelope like an anxious little kid receiving his first Christmas gift. To my surprise, the envelope had a check in it! The check had a total of $1,000 written on it. This was great - it put me at a total of $3,500 toward my school fees! I still had a lofty goal of raising $26,500 more, but I was thankful, since it was $1,000 I didn't have before. I looked at the name on the check to see who had sent it.

Remember that public profession I made in church the day before? The late Sir Albert Miller, to whom I had written a financial request letter, was in the church congregation that day. He was one of those who had called me into his office and nicely explained why he wouldn't be able to assist me with my school fees at the time. However, something had touched his heart at the last minute. I believe part of it was seeing me boldly profess my dreams of going off to UNC Charlotte in front of the entire church congregation, not knowing what my future would hold. May his soul rest in peace.

There I was, sitting on the airplane in a window seat, heading to Charlotte, North Carolina - a city in which I had never set foot, that I had only seen on television and maps. And now I would finally be there "in person, NOT TV" – as we say on the island. You can probably imagine that life is totally different on the island. Some islanders have never left the country, while some islanders have never left their island! Therefore, what many Americans see every day, we only see on TV, and we may NEVER go to these places we see on TV. So excited was I to be making this journey, I wanted to ask the lady sitting to my left to pinch me, so that I could wake up. Was I really on the plane going off to university? For the first time in my life, I was actually traveling far into the unknown, all alone, in the afternoon. At this point, I was numb; I could no longer feel the coconuts hitting my head. Everything was becoming real. Everyone thought I was crazy for even setting foot on that plane, but at that moment, crazy sure felt good to me.

As I stared out the window looking back at my small island where I was born and raised, Kelly Clarkson's song "Breakaway" echoed in my mind.

It occurred to me, in this moment, I was literally living out the words of this song I loved so much. My dreams were big and CRAZY for an island boy, but I was following them anyway on a ONE WAY ticket to Charlotte, North Carolina, not knowing what would happen in the weeks ahead. Leaving the island, I felt like I was moving out of the despair that the islanders accepted as their fate, and moving into the light of hope for my future… I was breaking away.

I was excited to finally be in this moment I had spent years waiting for. Still, the questions remained. What was going to happen when the plane landed? How would I make it through my first semester? How would I ever come up with my school fees? I did not quite know the answers.

Chapter 7 – Living on the Edge

Monday, August 16th, I remember getting out of the airplane at Charlotte Douglas International Airport. I was amazed at the size of the airport. I had never seen anything like it before. I felt like I was walking into the future. I would have not been surprised if I had been passed by kids on hoverboards like in the movie *Back to the Future II*. Looking back at that moment, I always laugh because you have not seen the future until you have been to Toronto's airport and other technologically advanced airports worldwide.

Now that I was off the plane, I was faced with the next challenge, finding my way out of the airport. I thought to myself, *Don't panic, Charlie! Just read the signs. OR just follow the lady who sat to the left of you on the plane, since she looked like she knew where she was going.* The signs looked too overwhelming to follow, so I chose to follow the lady. To this day, she probably remembers me as the "weirdo" who followed her all the way to the baggage claim area.

All of my Contiki friends were in stitches because they had seen larger airports and they could not relate to what I had experienced. To them, it sounded funny, but to a crazy island boy, it was terrifying.

After retrieving my baggage, I spotted Jessica Simpson, who held a sign up with my name on it. She was not Jessica Simpson, the famous celebrity, but Jessica Simpson, a UNC Charlotte student who picked me up, drove me to the university, and helped me get situated on campus. While we were riding in Jessica's car, which she named "Huberto," I remember passing so many gigantic cottonwood trees and forests. In all honesty, it was a bit frightening. I thought we were about to drive into the "middle of nowhere" like one of those scary movies I had seen in the past. Somehow, I was expecting every place in the USA to look like Miami, Florida, with lots of buildings and palm trees. I sat in the car, anticipating how life in college would be, wondering what else would be new and different to me, besides the trees.

On campus, I was one of the first students to check into the dorms, since I had to report to school earlier than everyone for the international students' orientation. The second person I met in Charlotte was my resident advisor, David. He was a well-built, muscular guy, who was very friendly and helped me get situated in my dorm room. I stayed on the 9th floor of the oldest and cheapest dormitory building on campus. Each room had two twin beds that could easily be converted to a bunk bed. The hall bathroom was shared between twelve guys. This was also new to me. I might not have grown up with a "silver spoon in my mouth," but I certainly didn't grow up sharing one bathroom with twelve guys. This was different for me, but I knew I wouldn't take too long to adjust. I went to bed that night with a lot on my mind. I wondered how the international students' orientation would be.

The next day, on Tuesday, August 17th, 2010, I reported to the orientation. With the help of my resident advisor and my campus map, I was able to find the building where the orientation would be held. We met in a huge lecture hall classroom where there were hundreds of new international students. I had never before met so many people from so many countries in one room. Among the countries represented were China, Japan, India, England, South Africa, Brazil, Ecuador, Nigeria, Australia, Jamaica, Bahamas of course, and so many more! Almost 100 nationalities were in that room! There were students from other countries I had never even heard of at the time, like Sri Lanka, and Bangladesh. It was amazing to hear the different accents and see how the different cultures interact with each other. While at the orientation, I also met a girl named Juanteria, who was from the Bahamas also. Her parents accompanied her to the orientation. We talked briefly and exchanged contact information.

The orientation was very helpful. We learned many tips to help us adjust to American culture. We were also given the expectations and requirements to maintain our legal student status in the USA. Sitting beside me were three British girls from London; their names were Nicola, Hannah Banana, and Natalie. I was so fascinated by their British accent. I suddenly had a great idea. This would be a perfect time for me to practice my British accent I had learned from one of my favorite movies, *Harry Potter*. During our "meeting new people icebreaker," I put on my best *Harry Potter* British accent, and said, "Hello, I'm Charles Rose from the Bahamas." Before, they could even respond properly, they burst out into laughter. They were obviously not expecting that! They introduced themselves and asked me more questions about my country and about myself.

Before the icebreaker ended, I asked them in my mock British accent, "Would you like to have a cup of tea?" They told me they most certainly would like to have a cup of tea with me sometime. I replied to them, "How lovely! We will have tea with the queen." My new British friends were laughing in tears. They stuck with me through the entire orientation and introduced me to the other new British students. I called the British students, "Brits." The "Brits" liked me, and among them was Sam, who later became one of my best friends. He was quite fascinated with my Bahamian accent as well. Sam was an exchange student from London studying Architecture. We related on so many different levels of life. In high school, I studied Computer Architectural Drafting for three years. This was one of the fields I considered getting into before I decided to study Civil Engineering.

After the orientation, we went back to our dorms. Ironically, Sam's dorms and mine were right across from each other, while everyone else's dorms were nearly 15-20 minutes away from ours. We headed back together. For the first time, I felt so alive. I felt at home.

That night, I lay down in my dorm room, staring out my window, wondering where I would be a week and a half later when all of my school fees were due. I could not sleep that night. So I got up and began reading my new book from Mrs. Rolle once again. It was very inspiring. It was about a married couple who didn't have much money at all, but they had faith in God for everything, including their dream home. Peggy's inspiring story gave me hope to accomplish my dream because I didn't have the money to fund my dreams either. I thought, *if God would do it for them, certainly He would do it for me.* Although I had initially thought Mrs. Rolle was giving me a scholarship check, she gave me something more powerful – rather than the gift of money, she gave me the gift of faith. This kept me going at a time when it was much needed.

Sam invited me everywhere he went with the Brits. He was very good at using maps to find his way around campus, while I was very good at getting lost on our huge campus. I constantly relied on my maps and Sam for direction. Sam and I went to nearly every campus event and nearly every college party. But thank God I was with Sam, who taught me how to party responsibly. He was a year ahead of me and had done it all, or at least he had done many things in his lifetime. He told me to have fun and avoid making mistakes. He believed in enjoying life, following his dreams, and not being afraid to take risks. He would always say, "The only shots you have missed in life are the ones you did not take."

All the while, I kept getting calls from home, notifying me of all the scholarships that had rejected me. It was kind of depressing being rejected from so many scholarship organizations, but I relied on my faith in God, somehow believing I wouldn't be disappointed. Again, I was very thankful to Mrs. Rolle for giving me Peggy's book. It gave me much-needed hope that really fueled my faith at a desperate time.

The next morning, I went to my first set of classes and met my new professors. One of those classes was an advanced math course, Calculus 1. I felt extremely lost in that class, especially when Ms. Birdsong, my professor, began talking about finding the derivatives of "logs." The first thing I thought in my mind was *Derivative?* And *what in the world do logs have to do with Mathematics?* Many of the students knew at least pre-calculus because they had done it in high school or some college prep program. There are only a handful of schools in the Bahamas that offer college prep classes. Those schools tend to be more expensive with more wealthy kids. I went to public school all my life, and we did not have any college prep programs that I knew of in our public school system in the Bahamas. So, many of the Americans were following along with what Ms. Birdsong was talking about. But I was lost and could only associate logs with tree logs. I had no idea how to take a derivative of a log, whatever that was. I knew that I was going to need a tutor if everything worked out with my school fees.

Although I had no idea what was about to happen, I was sure glad that I was taking classes at UNC Charlotte rather than the College of the Bahamas (COB). I believe COB has a good academic program; however, American degrees are more recognized worldwide. My mother inspired me from a young age to make my mark on the world, and I intended to accomplish that dream.

After class, I ran into Juanteria and her parents in the cafeteria, and we ate lunch together. She was the island girl I had met at the International Students Orientation. Her parents left us eating together, and went back to their hotel. They were very nice. Her father was a pastor, and her mother was a minister of the gospel. Juanteria and I connected on so many different levels since we were both from the Bahamas. She spoke to me about her life growing up on the island in Eleuthera. We spoke about how different the cafeteria food was compared to the food at home. The foods were very different in the way they were seasoned. Most of the cafeteria food tasted very bland compared to our richly-flavored island food. As unhealthy as it may be, we had to add a little bit more salt and pepper to give our food more flavor in the cafeteria.

After a long lunch, we decided to take a nice walk across campus together. While walking together, we compared life in the Bahamas to life in the USA. We also spoke about our dreams. She was studying to become a doctor, while I was studying to become an engineer. It was getting late, so we headed to the dorms, taking a short cut through the woods on campus. Before we parted ways, she invited me to go with her to the 11:00 AM service at a local church called University City Church. How could I say no? It was hard to for me to say no to a beautiful girl, especially one with whom I connected.

I woke up at 10:00 AM, freshened up, and was on the church bus at 10:15 AM with Juanteria for the 11:00 AM service. University City Church was a local growing church pastored by Dr. Michael & Sharon Stevens. To this day, I still remember that sermon. The message was, "If it is to be, then it is up to me." Dr. Stevens spoke about how we must do our part in order for faith to work. He spoke about trusting in God but not being lazy and expecting God to do everything for you. That sermon resonated with me deeply. It gave me a bit more confidence that I was doing the right thing by taking a step of faith to go off to school. But there was still one problem - my school fees were due in 3 days. I thought to myself, *What do I have to lose? Why give up on my faith now? After all, if it is to be, then it is up to me.* I spoke to Dr. Stevens after church and briefly shared my dilemma with him. He told me he would call me the next day.

The next day, Dr. Stevens kept his commitment and called me. He encouraged me to keep my faith alive and journal my entire journey in the USA. I appreciated that this man of God would take the time to mentor me in this way; so I followed his instructions and began writing. To this day, I'm so thankful Juanteria invited me to church. Juanteria and I did not end up together, but I believe that message was tailor-made for me. It's amazing how God used my attraction to Juanteria to lure me into hearing those much-needed words.

Now, it was the day before my school balance was due. Sam and I were taking a walk through the woods on campus when he asked me, "Bro, what made you come to the USA for university? Why would you ever want to leave the Bahamas?" I told him how I had always dreamt of studying abroad in the USA ever since I was a boy, selling snacks to save up money for college. I also shared with him that I did not know where I would be the next day if my school fees were not paid. I told him my story of all I went through to apply for university and scholarships. I told him I might be homeless if my school fees were not paid in time.

After letting me air out everything on my mind, Sam encouraged me. He said, "Don't worry brother, everything will work out! It always does. Besides, you can live in my dorm if they kick you out. You will get through this, brother." I felt so much better after hearing Sam's very encouraging words, although I could never have taken him up on his generous offer. I continued praying and believing that everything would work out.

So I was enjoying life in the USA, all the while having no idea what would happen to me once my school fees came due. In a short time, I would find out. Would the university keep me or kick me out? As the clock ticked, time was drawing closer and closer to the final hour.

At the final hour, I would know. Was it all a crazy, impossible dream? Or would the crazy island boy get to pursue his degree at his American university. Would things work out for me, or not?

Chapter 8 – The Final Hour

In no time at all, the day came that I had been dreading – September 1st, 2010. It was a fresh afternoon when I left my calculus class to go to my dorm to eat lunch and take a nap. When I opened my door, however, I found a note lying on the floor.

I will never forget this day.

It was a note from the university that brought reality into existence. This note was the coconut of all coconuts. It was like a STORM of HUGE coconuts, falling from the sky like hail, obliterating my head. Here is a copy of the note below:

> *Dear Charles,*
> *This serves as a final notice to pay all and any remaining charges on your account. Failure to do so will result in the cancelation of your house tonight September 1, 2010. For more information, please check your email, as multiple notices have been sent to you.*

This was just a fancy way of saying, "Pay your school fees today, or you will be kicked out tonight!" I still remember this moment today and I keep this note in my wallet as a symbol of my faith and where I came from.

I had never felt so hopeless before. I had given everything I had, my time, my effort, and all my money. For many years, I had always worked hard to maintain stellar academic performance and positive involvement in my community. I worked in the heat - whether it was landscaping in the sun, or flipping burgers in the kitchen - to save up for college. Then I spent my entire life savings on the college application process, and I couldn't see the reward I labored for all those years. What would I do if I went back home? Certainly, I would be an embarrassment to my family, I thought. On the island, especially in the Bahamas and other Caribbean destinations, the communities are small - everyone and their great-grandma knew your business. **People gossiped, ESPECIALLY island people.**

I was 17 years old, and I was about to become homeless.
I didn't know what else to do, except hide myself under my covers and cry. I almost gave up. I knew now that it would take a miracle to get me out of the jam I was in.

As I paused in my story to reflect on this awful memory, I could see watery eyes and teardrops in many of my Contiki friends' eyes, especially the tour guide, Christina.

So, I got down on my knees and prayed. It was the only thing left for me to do. I reminded God of how His word said, "I can do all things through Christ who strengthens me" (Philippians 4:13). I also reminded God that I had no reason to be disappointed since I trusted in Him, and gave everything I had to go to University. My phone rang, but I didn't answer it. Why bother? I then checked my voicemail, which was from my stepmother, Patrice. She told me I had another letter that came to our mail in the Bahamas.
This could only be another scholarship rejection letter, I thought to myself. I had heard so many "no's" by now.

...or, maybe, it could be something great... I decided to finish listening to the voice mail. What else was there to do? To my great astonishment, I heard her say, "You received a $7,500 grant from the Bahamas Government."

My heart dropped straight to my underwear. I said, "I received what?" Then I called back, and my family and I shouted and rejoiced over the phone. I told them I'd better get that letter to the student accounts office immediately to avoid cancellation of my housing and classes. I knew this wasn't enough to cover the remaining fees; however, I thought that certainly a letter from the Bahamas Government was my ticket to stay in the USA longer.

Soon thereafter, someone knocked on my door. It was Sam just stopping by to say hello. I was still rejoicing, and I squeezed Sam with a tight hug, telling him what happened. I then asked him how he knew everything would work out. He replied, "I just knew it would. It just always does, brother." I told him I would have to catch up with him later because I needed to take care of my school fees immediately!

By this time, it was about 4:30 PM in the afternoon. I remember running to the student accounts office from my dorm to submit the grant letter before the office closed at 5:00 PM. Luckily, this office was only about 5 minutes away. I was breathing hard when I arrived at the black counter top at the cashier's window. Behind the glass window was the same cashier who served me when I submitted my $2,000 Port Authority scholarship, the $500 check from the Coopers, and the $1,000 check from Sir Albert Miller. After catching my breath, I slid the copy of the letter from the Bahamas Government through the window. I told her, "Look, I have some money coming in from the Bahamas Government towards my school fees. I know it's not enough. Can you please give me more time to pay the remaining fees?" The lady looked over the letter for about one minute. My heart was beating so fast, it was just about ready to jump out of my chest. Finally, she said, "Okay, I will save your housing and classes from being canceled, but you have to pay the remaining school fees by November in order to register for your spring semester classes." At this point, I was not worried about the next semester; I just wanted to get through the current semester! I was happy and relieved that I would not be homeless. This certainly brought me another step closer to my dreams! I thanked the lady and went back to my dorm more joyful than ever.

The next morning, my mom's boss, Mr. Farrington, found out what had happened. Immediately he made a money transfer of $4,000 to my account, which was enough to cover the remaining balance of my school fees for that semester. What a miracle! I felt like I was on cloud nine! Coming from almost nothing, I was super-thankful. It felt almost like going from the "pit to the palace." It was truly a good semester. I went to all my classes, met new friends, enjoyed my first college parties, and I even joined the Jujitsu club! Despite the odds, everything worked out that semester.

"What happened next, Charlie?" were the words I heard from nearly all of my Contiki friends at the dinner table. Some of them had not even finished their food; they were so engrossed in the story. Keep reading on to find out.

Chapter 9 – Christmas Break and Broke Again

I had the best time ever that semester; however, I was faced with an even bigger problem in December of 2010. Only half my school fees were paid. The next half, about $15,000, was due on January 5th, 2011. The $2,000 Grand Bahamas Port Authority scholarship was only given once a year in the fall, while government grants and sponsor checks were not subject to renewal. Here is the other problem – I only had about $4 remaining in my bank account after I gave an offering in the basket at University City Church. My bank account was nearly empty, but my faith was full. My dad was able to scrape money together to purchase me a one-way airplane ticket from Charlotte to Freeport, Bahamas, to spend the Christmas break at home with my family.

I left about 75% of my belongings in Charlotte. I thought, *Everyone on the island called me "Crazy," so I might as well live up to my new name. I did it before; I could do it again. I could make it through the next semester.*

Christmas break was about three weeks long. I had a wonderful time with family and friends, and everyone asked me about my experience going off to school. I shared with them the wonderful time I had and many of the obstacles I faced to get through the first semester. I met up with my high school best friend Keron and shared with him how I learned to take the "derivatives of logs" in my calculus class. Keron had the same response I initially had, "The derivatives of what? How are tree logs associated with math? Boy, you better stop talking foolishness." We both laughed and continued catching up and reminiscing on the good old days.

Christmas that year was one of the best ever! We did a comedic family Christmas play directed by my sister, Chardonae. The family laughed and loved it so much and wanted us to do it again. This Christmas break, in particular, was one of the best because we hadn't had a very good family Christmas since Grampy, my mom's father, passed away in December 2004. Six years later, we were finally bringing the spirit of Christmas back. Grampy was always the one to keep the family together and made sure everyone had what they needed. Had he been alive, he would have made sure I had the resources I needed for college. But still, it was almost as if he were my guardian angel watching over me, because no matter how tough things got, everything seemed to work out for my good at the end of the day.

About two weeks into the Christmas break, I still only had $4 on my bank account. Nearly all my family and friends on the island told me I got lucky the first semester, and that I should have just went to the College of the Bahamas. They told me I was wasting time and money. I went to the Port Authority for extra assistance. They told me that they were not able to assist further. An official responsible for the program at that time told me, "Charles, I understand that studying in the USA is your dream, but it is just not possible right now. NO ONE gives scholarships in the Spring Semester. It just does not happen that way." I thanked her for her time and left. I thought to myself, *She must not know my God.* After I saw what crazy faith could do for me the first semester, why stop being crazy now? Crazy brought me another step closer to my dreams.

Two "crazy" things happened to me before New Year's Day. A reserved police officer from Freeport heard about my story of how I went off to school on a one-way ticket. He added me on Facebook and told me how proud he was to see young Bahamian men following their dreams. About two days before New Year's Day, this reserved police officer told me to check my email. At the top of my emails, I saw that he had sent me a one-way plane ticket back to Charlotte with my name on it. What was happening? I only had $4 in my account, and a ticket back to Charlotte, North Carolina. The first time I went off on a one-way ticket back in August 2010, I at least had $3,500 and money for my books. Whatever miracle was going to happen, it had to be the biggest one of them all!

Suddenly, Mrs. Rolle connected me with her daughter, Shasheena Rolle to do a TV interview. Shasheena also had to overcome financial obstacles when she went off to university to become a journalist. Through persistence and the power of God, she was able to complete her degree and become a news anchor at ZNS, the largest TV network in the Bahamas. She is truly one of the best journalists I know. At first, I declined Mrs. Rolle's offer. I told her I wasn't comfortable going on TV and begging for money. She told me that I wouldn't be begging for money on TV, but sharing my story of how I went off on "crazy faith" to accomplish my dreams. She told me it would encourage other young people to follow their dreams. I finally accepted the interview invitation.

Suddenly, I thought to myself, *Well, by golly! What will I say on national TV in front of everyone? What words should I use to encourage the young people? God, I hope I don't say anything stupid on TV!*

It was New Year's Eve 2010, in the afternoon, around 3:00 PM when Shasheena called me to do an interview. She stopped by my home and interviewed me in the living room. I sat on our living room chair in front of our bookshelf. The transcript of the interview is below.

The Interview

Shasheena: Charles Rose, a recent graduate from Jack Hayward High School, knows what it means to defy the odds. He is service-oriented and community-minded. He served as a member of the Interact club, graduated top of his class as head boy and decided to further his education. Charles Rose was accepted at the University of North Carolina, but he has had his share of challenges.

Charles: Being the first in my family to actually go off to study abroad in the U.S. was actually very challenging. My parents didn't know anything about applying in the U.S., so I basically had to do it all alone and they encouraged me all that they could, and it was very difficult going off because we're not in any financial position. But I just kept believing and I went off in faith and I prayed about it a lot and everything worked out for the first semester.

Shasheena: Worked out may be an understatement! In his first semester, Charles beat out his entire freshman class and attained a 4.0 major GPA. He's already making a difference in the United States.

Charles: During my first college semester, I kept my involvement in community service. I joined a community service club called Impact, and we did a lot of community service in the community helping out different youth organizations. I also was accepted as a part of an organization called Emerging Leaders.

Shasheena: While Rose is making a name for himself as a brilliant student internationally, there is one major problem. He may not be able to register for his upcoming classes.

Charles: I certainly have financial challenges going back to school, but I intend to just keep my faith going. I believe that someone out there may be able to help me, and I don't know who, but I'm just going to keep the faith.

Shasheena: He believes there are lots of students facing the same challenge. Charles said despite the odds, he has great plans for the future

Charles: One of my main goals is to help other young kids who are in the same position as I am because I know how hard it is to keep your focus, and how hard it is to have faith when you know you don't have enough money for school. But I intend to do anything I can to help others like me in the future.

Shasheena: Shasheena Rolle Zed-N-S news.

After the interview, the last thing Shasheena told me was, "Charles, I know what you're going through. When I went off to school, every semester I did not know if I would be able to return. We will get you every penny you need for school."

Visit **https://www.youtube.com/watch?v=7X4nsLr7sY8** to see the full interview.

Shasheena went back to work excited to air the interview on national TV. However, her supervisor had no interest in airing my interview. She told Shasheena, "We just don't air interviews like this." Shasheena was determined to air my interview that same day. She begged her supervisor until she succumbed, and allowed her to air the interview that evening. And Shasheena was right.

Immediately after being on air, people from the Bahamas and different parts of the world began calling the TV station, wondering how they could help this young man they had seen in the interview to achieve his dreams.

Captain Randy Butler, CEO of SkyBahamas, ensured that my story was further heard nationally and internationally. Shasheena interviewed him about his interest in assisting me. He gave a powerful statement, "My purpose is to help young people realize their dreams."

There were SO many people who prayed for me and invested into my education. Some people only gave a dollar; other people gave thousands of dollars. And some people just prayed for me. To this day, I am humbly thankful for them all. There was a wave of prayers and giving across the country. At a young age, I witnessed a nation come together – spiritually and financially - to help a 17-year-old young island boy achieve his dream. With the help of these generous donors, I was able to pay for my entire education at UNC Charlotte.

To this day, I keep a "gratitude list" of over 50 individuals who have consistently prayed for me and funded my education; I always send thank you notes to them. There was always an overflow of money, even when all funds came in later than expected. Oftentimes, I was able to shift thousands of additional dollars into the next semester.

Despite my challenges, everything worked out. On May 10th, 2014, I graduated UNC Charlotte with honors attaining a Bachelor of Science degree in Civil Engineering. At graduation, I had the honor of being the student graduation speaker. In my speech, I encouraged everyone to be crazy, if crazy meant being successful.

Photo of Charles Rose Jr Speaking at UNC Charlotte Graduation 2014 (Bruton, 2014)

People often ask me how I did it. I tell everyone the same thing. To accomplish my dream, all I needed was the following 3 G's:

1. God (keep believing)
2. Grades (keep a high GPA)
3. Givers (Keep them updated and thank them)

"So this is my story in a nutshell. Purchase the book in a few months if you would like to hear the full story," I told my new Contiki friends at the dinner table in Monaco. Everyone at the table was so moved emotionally; some of them were in tears. Many of them had come from well-off families. In fact, one of them has grandparents who have a luxury home in the Bahamas. Many had told me to write my story over the years. But it wasn't until sitting in front of this group that I fully realized that the world needed to hear my story. After traveling a part of the world, I have come to the realization that it's not about my story; it's about the next story - your story.

From the table at Pizza Hut in Grand Bahama where I was told the world is not just the Bahamas, to the table in Monaco, to the conference table of one of the largest construction companies in the world where I oversee many large civil engineering projects, this is my story of dreams, perseverance, hope, and faith in God. It all starts with a dream - believe and have faith.

Continue Reading Parts 2 & 3 and take action!
I want to hear your story next!

Part 2: Keys

Chapter 10 - Summary of Key Points

In this chapter, I will summarize seven key points from my story that helped me during my journey.

1. **Dream Big** – *Don't Stop Believing*
    Everyone has a dream. Don't stop dreaming, especially when your dream seems impossible. Remember - your dream is all you have at this point. What are you dreaming about? What is on your heart? What do you want to do that people would not believe? What are you dreaming that scares you? Your dream must be big enough to be passionate about. And remember, don't just dream big; you need to act big also.

2. **Tell Yourself to Shut Up!** – *Listen to Your Intuition*
    One day my good friend Kesha from Have Life Church in Charlotte, North Carolina, told me, "Charles, tell yourself to shut up!" Immediately, my mouth dropped in surprise. "What do you mean tell myself to shut up?" I asked as if she were crazy. I thought I had said something to offend her. She then said, "In order for you to make it, in order for you to follow your dreams, you have to tell yourself to shut up." What she was saying was don't let your negative self-talk drown out the small, still voice of your intuition. Kesha ended the conversation by saying. "If you can't tell yourself to shut up, who can?" I had to tell that negative self-talk

to shut up when I was standing before my church, making a public declaration that I was going off to UNC Charlotte.

3. **Walk in Purpose** - *Trial & Error*
We were all designed with a purpose. Sometimes, it takes a while to discover it. Do you know your purpose? Dr. Myles Munroe, a Bahamian and world-renown bestselling author once said, "The greatest tragedy in life is not death, but a life without purpose." In order to find your purpose, ask yourself three questions, (a) What is your passion? (b) What annoys you most? and (c) What makes you alive?
The answers to these questions comprise what you are called to solve - it is your purpose. What if you don't know the answers to these questions or you are not quite sure? Sometimes, we have to go through trial and error to discover our purpose. We have to figure out what works, what doesn't work, what we like, and what we dislike. I learned this concept from my Pastor, Shomari White, who teaches people how to find their purpose. Join different organizations to feel what they do. See if you like it. Start the business you are thinking about doing with what you have. My sister and I had our first business shut down because we were selling our snacks without being an authorized vendor. Am I encouraging you to do unconventional actions to find your purpose? Yes, as long as they are not against the laws of your government or the laws of God. What is your purpose?

4. **Go off** – *Face the Unknown with Faith*
I remember before going off to university, I had NO idea where to start! Faith is the only thing that kept me going during this process. I was stepping into the realm of the unknown. I believe in Saint Augustine's definition of *faith*, "Faith is to believe what you do not

see; the reward of this faith is to see what you believe." Seeing what you believe is the best reward ever. I could not naturally see where I was going, but I saw myself going off in my dreams. Going off to university and the steps to get there were TOTALLY new to me; I had only been there in my mind. I felt like Indiana Jones stepping off a cliff in search of the Holy Grail. We often go off into many unknown situations in our lives. We must take these risks in order to achieve our dreams, and turn our vision for our lives into our reality. Where are you dreaming of going? Go off to achieve that dream! Remember, *"In order to get something you never had, do something you've never done."*

5. **Seek Assistance** – *Don't be afraid to scream for help!*
   This step was hard for me, especially when I was shy. I was so used to doing everything on my own that I was too prideful to ask for help. This is something my mentor, Dr. Robinson always taught me. He would say, "Son, think of yourself highly, but not more than you ought to." The first step after dreaming big is the art of humility. Only through humility will you be open to learn and take on new opportunities. Only through humility will others want to help you fulfill your dreams. Only through humility, will you truly be successful. Being humble is the first step to opening the doors of favor in your life. When the doors of favor open in your life, people will find you and help you fulfill your dreams. If I had not been humble and refused to be interviewed on national TV by Shasheena, I would not be writing this book. Please know that you are never in anything alone. We need help to carry on. Find me one successful person who did it on his or her own. You can't! They will tell you people helped them along the way, and people still help them to this day. Sending out financial request letters and going on TV to

seek assistance was the hardest thing for me to do. What helped me overcome my resistance was the thought that in sharing my story, I would be encouraging other young people. I needed people's help not only financially but also intellectually and spiritually. There were many people whom I asked for advice during the university and scholarship application process. There were many people whom I just asked to pray for me. I believe that prayer was the most powerful thing I could ever have ask for.

If you are in high school, seeking assistance from your guidance counselor is a great place to start. If you have not done so already, schedule the next available appointment. Your guidance counselor can help you reach your dream.

6. **Be Thankful** – *Gratitude determines your latitude!*
   As a young boy in Sunday school hearing The Ten Lepers Bible story, I learned one great message from that story that stuck with me for life- **Always say thank you**. In the story, Jesus healed ten men who had suffered with leprosy and only one of the ten turned around to say thank you. After hearing this story, I told myself that I always want to be like the man who turned back to say thank you. **Zig Ziglar said, "Your attitude, not your aptitude, will determine your latitude."** I'd like to even go a step further and say, *Your gratitude determines your latitude*. What you are thankful for today will keep flowing back your way. It is very important to be thankful for all that you receive. I remembered what my uncle Pancake said: "Nobody owes you anything, not even your parents" Verbally expressing your thanks is important, but go a step further and send thank you notes (email would be fine, but thank you cards are even better). I promise you that

this will make your gratitude responses even more powerful. Gratitude not only empowers you, but it also empowers the one receiving the thanks – the giver. Your thankfulness energizes the giver to continue giving, especially when they have a thank you note they can go back to; this note reminds them of the difference they are making. One of my college supporters, Mrs. Grant, keeps a file on me in her law office with all of my thank you notes. Her employees laugh, but she smiles and reads through every one of those notes regularly from time to time.

With this being said, thank you for reading this - my first book!

7. **Pay It Forward** – *Help somebody else!*
   When you achieve your goals and dreams, help somebody else achieve theirs. Don't be selfish. Paying it forward is so important, even for you to move forward and fulfill your purpose. I encourage you to always tithe your time, talent, and treasure. You can start right now from where you are. Ways you can help others include volunteering your time with an organization, serving at your church, giving to an organization, giving to your church, being a listening ear to those in need, or helping someone to get through what you went through. There are so many ways you can pay it forward. One of the biggest ways I am paying it forward is through a mentoring & scholarship organization, which a team and I are launching in 2017. Our vision is simply to help young people realize their dreams. Captain Randy Butler, CEO of SkyBahamas, and many others helped me to realize my dream of a college education, so I am paying it forward by helping other people realize their dreams. Part of the proceeds of this book will go into the organization's scholarship

fund. Plan to pay it forward; it will change lives. You can start making a difference right where you are with what you have.

These seven key points will help you achieve your personal dream. If you dream big, listen to your intuition, walk in purpose, go off, seek assistance, be thankful, and pay it forward **YOU WILL BE SUCCESSFUL** in all you do.

But of course, before you can follow these steps, first you must know your dream. A dream starts from a vision. In the remaining two chapters, I will help you understand put your dream in words, write it down, and take action.

Part 3: Call to Action

Chapter 11 – Dream Template

One of the most important things I did was writing my dreams on paper.

Benjamin Franklin once said, "If you fail to plan, you plan to fail." It is very important for you to plan your future.
The purpose of this chapter is for you to write what your dream is and write down the steps to get there.

Go ahead and fill out each category in the template below

Dream – Write down your dream. Focus on the part of it that you want to achieve or get started within the next year. You can use this template for short-term and/or long-term planning. For example, my dream was to obtain a Civil Engineering degree from an accredited university in the USA. What is yours?

Purpose – Your purpose is whatever you are passionate about - something you do that fulfills you most. It is something that motivates you. It explains why you exist. (Manson, n.d.) You may feel you have multiple purposes; if you have to choose one, what would it be? What would you love to do for free?

Obstacles – These are things that can be potential barriers, or things you feel are blocking you from your dreams. Typical barriers are things like money, education, fear, and time. Identifying your obstacles and writing them down beforehand helps you to address potential barriers early on so that you can create ways to overcome them.

Goals & Steps – Write down your goals and the steps necessary to achieve them. Be sure that your goals follow the SMART goals system. They should be specific, measurable, attainable, realistic, and timely. For example, one of my goals for achieving my dream of obtaining a Civil Engineering degree was to go to college. One of the attainable and realistic steps to getting there was applying to different universities. To be specific with this goal, I would say: apply to universities that offer "Civil Engineering." To be measurable, I would say: apply to at least three universities. To be even more specific and measurable I can add a timeline. I can say: "My goal is to apply to four universities that offer Civil Engineering by March 8th of next year." You can see how this is a SMART goal, as it is specific, measurable, attainable, realistic, and timely.

Mentor – Who would be a good mentor to help you achieve your dreams? It is always good to find a mentor who is already successful at what you want to do. I was fortunate to be mentored by Dr. Byron Robinson throughout college, who is a former College Dean in the State of North Carolina. He helped me achieve my dreams of obtaining a Civil Engineering degree, and became a surrogate father to me in the USA. I call him my American Dad. In some cases, you may not be able to find your mentor right away. However, be on the lookout for a mentor who will at least encourage you and show you when you are heading in the wrong direction. Listen to him or her. It will pay off in the long run if you listen and act on your mentor's positive words.

I have prepared the following Dream Template to help you fulfill your dream.

Dream Template
Name:

_____

Purpose – What are you passionate about?

_____
_____

Obstacles - What are you afraid of? OR What can impact your goals?

_____
_____

Goals & Steps – specific and measurable

1. Goal:_____
   a. Steps:_____
      _____
      _____
      _____

2. Goal:_____
   a. Steps:_____
      _____
      _____
      _____

3. Goal:_____
   a. Steps:_____
      _____
      _____
      _____

4. Goal:_____
   a. Steps:_____
      _____
      _____
      _____

FIND A MENTOR – Who would be a good mentor to help you reach your dream?

_____

Don't skip this section! This will help you achieve your dreams. Remember, Benjamin Franklin once said, "If you fail to plan, you are planning to fail."

Refer to "The Ultimate Guide to Success" and the "The Life You Want Workbook" by Dan McDaniel for an interactive template.

Great job - your plans are now on paper! The next section will give you motivation to get started. One more chapter! You can do it!

Chapter 12 – Where Do I Go Next?

Now that you have written down your dreams, identified your obstacles, your goals, and the steps needed to achieve them, you may be wondering, "Where do I go next? How do I successfully achieve my goals?" I can totally relate to those questions. My dreams may be different from your dreams, but our dreams share one thing. There are lots of unknowns.

Like my mom told me, "google it!" And as Mr. Derreck Farquharson told me, "Do the 3 W's.

Ask yourself the 3 W's, plus the 4th W (introduced below) and get started! Don't delay! The sooner you get started, the sooner you'll realize your dreams.

Remember the 3 W's. These three things can get you to your goal, through your goal, and through life.

The 3 W's

1. What do I know?

    _____

    _____

2. What can I find out?

    _____

    _____

3. Who can I ask?

    _____

    _____

The 4th W

Where do I want to be?

Remember what my mom did with the map of the world in the beginning? I encourage you to do the same. Where you are right now is one little dot on the map? Discover where you need to be. Are you there now? Do you need to be somewhere else?

Print a copy of the map of the world. Place a dot where you are and, place an X where you need to be. It is okay if you have more than one X. Put this somewhere you can see it daily (your bathroom mirror, closet door, or refrigerator) as a reminder of where you are headed. Every day, do something toward your dream. Ask yourself, "Am I doing things to add to my dream or subtract from my dream?"

Now you're ready to go out there and chase your dreams. I've shared my story to encourage you to go and begin yours.
The world is waiting to hear your journey to success. You can defy odds and realize your dreams. Remember, "It's not about my story; it's about the next story - your story"
And now, a word from my most important mentor, my mother...

Message to Mothers

By Chassarie Sealy-Bullard, Mother of Charles (CJ) Rose Jr.

We were all sitting on the back porch of my good friend, Rotary President Carol Rolle, eating, drinking, and dancing to simply celebrate - something we do best on the island. Carol had her closest family and friends over at her home to celebrate her being the 48th President for the Rotary Club of Lucaya. I had always prayed for God to send people like Carol Rolle, to be a good example in my children's life.

Suddenly, I heard her daughter Shasheena make a statement that made me remember the hard days raising my son. Shasheena said, "I just can't see Charles doing any wrong. He must have been easy to deal with growing up!" I was stunned by her words: I told her, "Not my son! Not CJ! (Our family calls Charles, CJ, since he is a Junior). While raising CJ, I had to get on my knees many nights and pray because of how hard it was. He challenged everything I told him. I remember him reverting to his shyness and slamming doors, being stubborn, and wanting to do everything his way." I could see CJ looking embarrassed, as he tapped my leg under the table, gently pleading with me to leave the past alone. But I didn't say all of that to be negative about my son.

I am a mother of two amazing children, who are now budding successful adults. It takes sacrifice, dedication, work, and perseverance to raise a child. It takes great efforts to train a child in the way he/she should go, especially when you are a single mother.

I am very proud of CJ's accomplishments, especially his first "best-selling" book. He has given me the honor of ending this book with a "Message to Mothers." I have been blessed to have the help of mothers like Carol Rolle, Patrice Cooper, and many others who have played a significant role in helping me raise CJ into the great man he is today. People always ask me what I did and how I did it. My answers to them are always the same. I have summarized 7 keys to raising a child that worked for me:

1. **Transform Negative Energy into Positive Energy**
   If you are a mother, I am sure you can agree that raising kids is not easy. There are many seemingly negative characteristics your children may build at an early age that you want to get rid of. I learned to redirect negative energy into positive energy: I remember my daughter Chardonae always repeating the laws of physics around the house. It was annoying at first, but she was learning, and I did not want to stop that. One of her favorite physics laws was the law of conservation of energy – **"Energy can neither be created nor destroyed; rather it transforms from one form to another." She repeated this over and over again like a scorch record!** I thought to myself, "Aha! That is the answer." Instead of stopping my children from drawing on the walls, why not give them something to draw on. I explained to them in a simple way why I do not want them to draw on the walls and they understood. This method worked for me in so many other situations. It created a "win-win" with my children and myself.

2. Always Speak Life into Your Children

"Why are you so stupid? Why are you so ugly? Why are you so bad just like your_____?" I never spoke these to my children. I spoke life. I always tried to speak the pure, powerful, and the positive. Instead of calling them stupid, I would tell them, "You are too intelligent. Intelligent people don't do that." Instead of calling them ugly, I always called them handsome or beautiful. Instead of telling them they are bad, I tell them they are good and they should not be anything other than good. It was not easy but I had to find creative ways to build my children up rather than tear them down with my words, especially when I was angered by their actions. Words have the ability to build or destroy. Choose them wisely, especially with your children.

3. Invest in Your Children

One of the greatest returns on investment is seeing the success of your children. Invest into your children at an early age. Take them on breakfast, lunch, and dinner dates (just you and them). Eat together at home. Make family decisions together. Watch movies together. Spend time with them and their friends; know who they are spending time with. Go to church together. Pray together. Be a part of whatever they are involved with. The investment of time in your children will pay the greatest returns on investment ever. This is something money cannot buy.

4. Make Do With What You Have

You don't have to be middle class or rich to give your children all they need. Teach your children to appreciate everything. Teach them how to set goals. Teach them about sacrificing to earn and achieve their goals. There is always a way for them to reach their goals – ALWAYS.

5. **Have Values and Principles**

Teach your children values and principles. I am a firm believer in "Training a child up in the way he/she should go, and even when he/she is old, he/she will not depart from it" (Proverbs 22:6). Train your children to love themselves, treat others as they would treat themselves, approach everything with fairness, and understand every angle. Train them to honor their words, to listen more than they speak, and develop stick-ability, meaning stick to what you decide to do and finish it. Even when they stumble in life, they will always remember how you trained them. There are countless times, now that they are adults, when my children come to me and say, "Mom I now see what you meant by "XYZ." When you first said it I did not believe or understand you, but now I do."

Through discipline, these key values and principles can be achieved. I always told my children there are consequences for every action. "Every action has a reaction." One time, I turned off the Internet for an entire school semester, since my children decided to play on the Internet and neglect their studies. That semester, they achieved the highest grades in their class. As a result of their achievements, I rewarded them by turning the Internet back on and reminding them to always put education first. They continued to keep their grades up, while the Internet stayed on.

6. You Make Your Bed; You Lay in It

I always believed in giving my children room to make their own decisions. Whether it was the best decision or not, I encourage them to honor their decision and be consistent. In 2006, my daughter Chardonae made the decision to apply for the Rotary Youth Exchange Program. She was accepted into the 2007/2008 year to go to Ecuador and learn more about their culture and language. A quarter way through the year, she got homesick and was ready to quit and come back home. I told her she had to honor her decision and complete the program. She did just that and stayed. By the end of the program, she was not ready to return home. There are times my children did not make the best choices; however, I always encouraged them to honor their decision and make the best of it.

7. **Kick the Bird out of the Nest**

   There comes a point when the mother bird has given the baby bird enough food and shelter; at this point, she kicks the baby bird out of the nest. The baby bird has to either fly or die. Most of them choose to fly. You must do the same for your children. You are the mother bird. Start preparing your children for adulthood in their teen years. Give them their allowance and lunch money at the beginning of the week, or the beginning of the month if possible. This teaches them to budget. Allow them to open up their own bank account; let them do their own deposits. Let them fill out their own application forms. Let them do their own research. I always tell them if they don't know, look it up in the dictionary or "google" it. Let them start at a young age so they can easily transition into adulthood. I know they are your babies, but you have to start preparing them to fly on their own. In order for your children to fly and soar high to accomplish their dreams, you have to "kick" them out of the nest. CJ puts it like this, "I see what you were doing, Mom. You had to let us go in order to let us grow."

These are the 7 keys I used to raise my children. If you transform negative energy into positive energy, always speak life into your children, invest in your children, make do with what you have, have values and principles, teach them to lay in the bed they make, and kick the bird out of the nest when it's time, YOU WILL have successful children. As I mentioned to Shasheena, CJ was not easy to raise - it took hard work. Thanks to the almighty God and my 7 successful keys, my son is a Civil Engineer who is now paying it forward by paving the way for others. He believes *it's not about his story, it's about the next story, your son's or daughter's story.*

About the Author

Charles Rose Jr. grew up in Freeport, Bahamas, in a very close-knit family. He holds a Bachelor of Science degree in Civil Engineering from the University of North Carolina at Charlotte. He has a passion for people and helping them realize their dreams. One day he plans to launch a worldwide mentoring and scholarship foundation. Part of the proceeds from his first best-selling book, *Journey to Success,* is dedicated to this foundation. For more information, please contact **journeytosuccesslaunch@gmail.com**.

Urgent Plea

Thank you for reading this book! I hope it inspired and energized you to accomplish your dreams.

Your feedback would be greatly appreciated.

Please leave a helpful review on Amazon about my book! Let me know your story also, I look forward to reading it!

Write it in your review or email me at journeytosuccesslaunch@gmail.com

Thank you!

References

Manson, M. (n.d.). 7 strange questions that help you find your life purpose. Retrieved from **http://markmanson.net/life-purpose**

McCabe, K. (2011, April 7). Caribbean immigrants in the United States. Retrieved from http:**//www.migrationpolicy.org/article/caribbean-immigrants-united-states**

William States Lee College of Engineering (2014, May 7). From the Bahamas to UNC Charlotte - Charles Rose's story of perseverance, faith and family. Retrieved from http://motorsports.uncc.edu/news/bahamas-unc-charlotte-charles-roses-story-perseverance-faith-and-family

Write to Learn (2014, June 2). 10 barriers to education around the world. Retrieved from **https://www.globalcitizen.org/en/content/10-barriers-to-education-around-the-world-2/**

Bruton, W. (2014). Photo of Charles Rose Jr Speaking at UNC Charlotte Graduation 2014 [Photograph].

www.ingramcontent.com/pod-product-compliance
Lightning Source LLC
La Vergne TN
LVHW051814080426
835513LV00017B/1949